Matter Close-Up

What is a solid?

by Lynn Peppas

Crabtree Publishing Company

www.crabtreebooks.com

Author
Lynn Peppas

**Publishing plan research
and development**
Sean Charlebois, Reagan Miller
Crabtree Publishing Company

Editor
Kathy Middleton

Proofreader
Wendy Scavuzzo

Photo research and graphic design
Katherine Berti

Print and production coordinator
Katherine Berti

Photographs by Shutterstock

Library and Archives Canada Cataloguing in Publication

Peppas, Lynn
       What is a solid? / Lynn Peppas.

(Matter close-up)
Includes index.
Issued also in electronic format.
ISBN 978-0-7787-0771-4 (bound).--ISBN 978-0-7787-0778-3 (pbk.)

       1. Solid state physics--Juvenile literature. 2. Solids--Juvenile
literature. I. Title. II. Series: Matter close-up

QC176.3.P47 2012   j530.4'1   C2012-904363-X

Library of Congress Cataloging-in-Publication Data

CIP available at Library of Congress

Crabtree Publishing Company

www.crabtreebooks.com   1-800-387-7650

Printed in Hong Kong/092012/BK20120629

Published in Canada
Crabtree Publishing
616 Welland Ave.
St. Catharines, Ontario
L2M 5V6

Published in the United States
Crabtree Publishing
PMB 59051
350 Fifth Avenue, 59th Floor
New York, New York 10118

Published in the United Kingdom
Crabtree Publishing
Maritime House
Basin Road North, Hove
BN41 1WR

Published in Australia
Crabtree Publishing
3 Charles Street
Coburg North
VIC 3058

Contents

Solid matter

Everything around you is made of matter. People, cars, water, clouds, and air are all different types of **matter**. Matter is anything that takes up space. Matter has **mass**. Mass is the amount of **particles**, or material, that something has.

Matter comes in three main **states**, or forms—solid matter, liquid matter, and gas matter. This book is about solid matter. Solid matter is something you can see, hold, and touch. Your pencil is solid. Your desk is solid. The plant on a windowsill is solid. So is the pot and soil it is planted in.

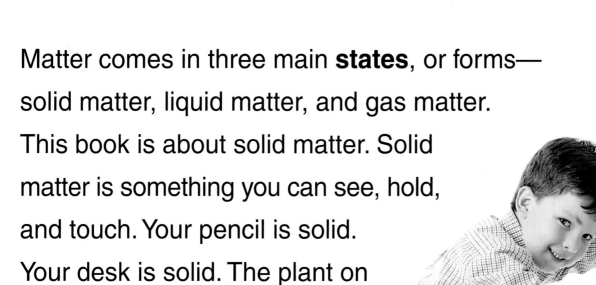

Why can you jump into water but not walk through a wall?

5

Talking about matter

States of matter have different **properties**. Properties are ways to describe how an object looks, feels, smells, or tastes. Properties are the qualities something has that makes it different from other things.

Solid Matter

A solid does not change its shape easily. Its shape stays the same when you move it from one container to another.

A marble does not change its shape when you move it from one container to another.

Liquid Matter

A liquid moves or flows easily. It takes the shape of the container it is in. It can be poured from one container to another easily.

A liquid such as orange juice takes the shape of the container it is in.

think?

Gas Matter

A gas, such as air, is something that is all around us but cannot be seen. Gas moves or flows easily. It takes the shape of the container it is in. Gas spreads out to take the shape of any container it is put in.

Which of these pictures show a solid, a liquid, or a gas?

7

In touch with matter

Solids have many different properties such as shape, size, color, and **texture**. Texture is how something feels. Some solids are hard, such as bike helmets. Some solids are soft, such as kittens. Even though they feel very different, they are both solid.

Solid shapes

A solid has its own shape. Most solids keep their shape even when put into different containers. You can change the shape of some solids if you try. Modeling clay is a solid that you can change the shape of. You can mold it into different shapes or flatten it out. But when you leave it alone, it stays in the same shape. Solids keep their shape unless you do something to change them.

It is difficult to change the shape of a hard solid, but it can be done. Solids such as paper can be ripped or cut. But, even if you do change them, they are still solids.

Dissolving a solid

Some solids **dissolve** when added to a liquid. Dissolve means to break up into very small pieces. Being able to dissolve in a liquid is a property that some—but not all—solids have. Sugar is a solid, but when pieces of sugar are added to water, they become so small you cannot see them.

Laundry detergent is a soap that dissolves in washing machines to clean clothes.

Add a spoonful of sugar to a small glass of liquid water and stir it. Where did the sugar go? Even though it looks as though the sugar is gone, it is still there. It has broken up into very small pieces that you cannot see. It has dissolved.

If you were to take a small sip of the water-and-sugar mixture, how do you think it would taste? Why?

11

Measuring up!

A solid can be measured in different ways. The size of a solid can be measured with a ruler or measuring tape. The mass of a solid is how much matter is in it. Mass is measured using a scale or **balance**. Solids with a small amount of matter, such as a feather, are lighter than solids with more matter, such as a school bus.

A solid always has the same **volume**. Volume is the amount of space an object takes up. A solid takes up the same amount of space in whatever container you put it into.

A baking recipe asks for one cup (240 ml) of sugar. Sugar is a solid. Why does the shape of sugar make it easy to measure its volume in a measuring cup?

Hint: One cup of sugar holds millions of tiny pieces of sugar.

Physical changes

Solids keep their shape unless you do something to change them. A **physical change** is when matter changes the way it looks. If you cut a piece of paper, you change the shape it is in. But it is still paper. It is still the same type of matter.

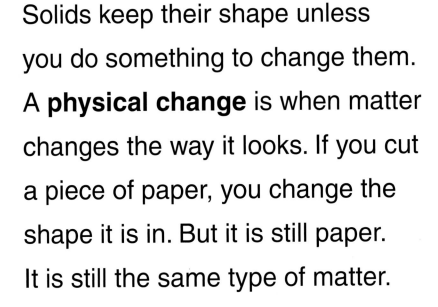

Adding energy to a solid can change the way it looks, too. Heat is a type of energy. A candle is made of solid wax. Heat from a flame changes the solid wax to liquid.

Some matter can be changed back after it has been changed. Candle wax will harden into a solid again when heat is removed from it. However, paper cannot be "uncut" after it is cut.

What do you think?

Put a solid ice cube from the freezer into a microwavable bowl. Heat it in the microwave for two minutes. Will the ice cube look different when you take it out? How will it look? What made it change?

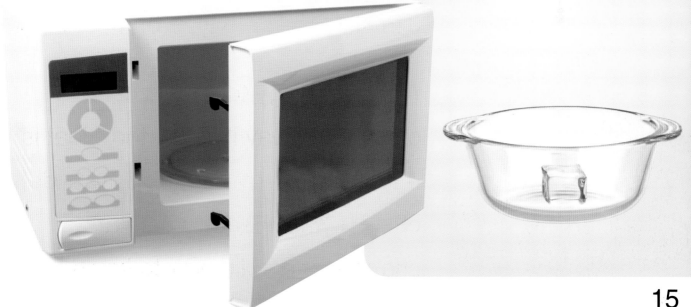

15

Melting

A change in temperature usually makes matter change its state. Solids change shape when they are heated. If enough heat energy is added, they change into a liquid. The temperature at which a solid changes to a liquid is called its **melting point**.

It is easier to change the state of some solids than others. Ice cream is a solid that turns to liquid just from the heat of your tongue! A solid such as iron is much harder to change. You have to add a lot of heat to iron to change it into a liquid.

The melting point of iron is 2,795 degrees Fahrenheit (1,535 degrees Celsius)!

What do you think?

Butter and pans are both solid matter. When an adult puts butter in a pan and turns the burner on underneath, the butter melts but not the pan. Why does the pan not melt, too?

Water changes

Water is a type of matter that changes state easily. At **room temperature**, water is liquid. When heat is added to water it becomes water **vapor**, or the gas state of water.

To turn liquid water into solid ice you must take heat away from it. Water freezes when its temperature reaches 32 degrees Fahrenheit (0 degrees Celsius). This is the **freezing point** of water. At this temperature, water changes from a liquid to a solid.

What do you think?

Have an adult put some ice cubes in a pot on the stove. Turn the burner on to add heat to the ice. What do you think the first change of state will be? As the pot gets hotter, what will the second change be?

The salt is still there

Even when a solid is dissolved in water, it is still a solid. This activity shows that even when the Epsom salts seem to have dissolved or disappeared—they are still there!

What do you think?

black or dark-colored construction paper

1/2 cup (120 ml) of warm water

4 tablespoons (60 ml) of Epsom salts

paintbrush

What to do:

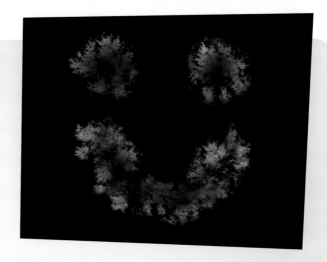

1 Add the Epsom salts to the warm water. Stir with the paintbrush.

2 Dip the paintbrush into the water-and-Epsom salts mixture.

3 Use your paintbrush to paint a smiley face picture (or whatever you wish) on the construction paper. (Hint: Do not soak the paper too much.)

4 Place the paper in a warm, dry place where it can dry.

What do you think?

When the water dries from your picture, all that will be left is the salty outline of your drawing. Epsom salts are solid. They dissolve in the water, which means they break into tinier pieces you cannot see. But they are still there. When the water is heated, it changes into water vapor so all that is left on your paper is the salt.

21

Useful solids

Solid objects are useful because they can keep their shape. Different types of solids have different properties that make them useful for certain jobs.

Wool is very soft. It keeps you warm and is comfortable to wear.

A hair clip is very light. It keeps hair neat and is not too heavy on your head.

Iron is very strong and is used in the construction of buildings.

Would you be able to sit in a chair if it were made of liquid water?

Learning more

Books

Amazing Materials (Amazing Science series)
by Sally Hewitt, Crabtree Publishing, 2008.

Changing Materials (Working with Materials series)
by Chris Oxlade, Crabtree Publishing, 2008.

Websites

www.linktolearning.com/grade2science.htm
A list of science websites that help explain the properties
of solids and liquids.

http://fossweb.com/modulesK-2/SolidsandLiquids/index.html
Use the virtual oven or freezer on this website to change
a liquid into a solid or a solid into a liquid.

www.harcourtschool.com/activity/states_of_matter
Find how particles in a solid, a liquid, or a gas behave
under a virtual microscope on this website.

http://e-learningforkids.org/Courses/EN/S0602/index.html
Mr. Beaker explains the three main states of matter, and
how and why they change on this fun, interactive website.

Glossary

Note: Some boldfaced words are defined where they appear in the book

balance [BAL-ans] *noun* A tool that measures the mass or weight of an object

freezing point [FREE-zing POYNT] *noun* The temperature at which a liquid changes into a solid

melting point [MEL-ting POYNT] *noun* The temperature at which a solid changes into a liquid

physical change [FIZ-i-kel CHAYNJ] *adjective and noun* A change in the way matter looks

property [PROP-er-tee] *noun* A special quality or attribute that a type of matter has

room temperature [RUME TEMP-er-a-chur] *adjective* Something that is the same temperature as the room it is in

A noun is a person, place, or thing. A verb is an action word that tells you what someone or something does. An adjective is a word that tells you what something is like.

Index